Virtue Politics:
Mencius on kingly rule

Translated by Mingyuan Hu

Hermits United
London · Paris

Published in Great Britain by Hermits United Ltd. 2023
English translation copyright © Mingyuan Hu 2023
Printed in Europe

This book is part of the Erstwhile Series
A catalogue record for this book is available
from the British Library
ISBN 978-1-7391156-1-6

www.hermits-united.com

Virtue Politics

372–289 BC

An advocate of Confucian morality, Mencius exhorted ruling through virtue during the Warring States, when sundry ideas of effectual governance prospered. Like Confucius had done two centuries before him, Mencius wandered from state to state, lobbying sovereigns. Mencian virtue politics has been pivotal to political thinking in China, though most appealing, it may be argued, to scholars. From *Mencius*, Mingyuan Hu selects and translates four dialogues exemplary of this thinking.

亦有仁義而已矣 11
Goodness and Honour Suffice 13

天下惡乎定 17
How May the World Be in Peace 20

保民而王 23
Protect the People 33

乃若其情、則可以為善矣 52
Following Nature,
People Are Able to Do Good 55

亦有仁義而已矣

孟子見梁惠王。王曰、叟不遠千里而來、亦將有以利吾國乎。孟子對曰、王何必曰利、亦有仁義而已矣。王曰何以利吾國、大夫曰何以利吾家、世庶人曰何以利吾身、上下交征利而國危矣。萬乘之國弒其君者、必千乘之家。千乘之國弒其君者、必百乘之家。萬取千焉、千取百焉、不為不多矣。苟為後義而先利、不奪不饜。未有仁而遺其親者也、未有義而後其君者也。王亦曰仁義而已矣、何必曰利。

Goodness and Honour
Suffice

Mencius was received by King Hui of Liang. The King asked: 'The old gentleman has travelled far to see me. Has he something to profit my state?'

Mencius replied: 'Why does the King speak of profits? Goodness and honour suffice. The King asks: "How to profit my state?" The ministers ask: 'How to profit my family?" The commoners ask: "How to profit myself?" High and low, all fight for profits and the state is in peril. In a territory of ten thousand chariots, he who kills the sovereign has a thousand. In a territory of a thousand chariots, he who kills the sovereign has a hundred. Where there are ten thousand, he has a thousand; where there are a thousand, he has a hundred. Not that his assets are scarce. Putting honour second and profits first, he is insatiate till he usurps. There has never been a good man who deserts his parents. Never has there been an honourable man who forsakes his sovereign. The King need only speak of goodness and honour. Why does he speak of profits?'

天下惡乎定

孟子見梁襄王。出、語人曰、望之不似人君、就之而不見所畏焉。卒然問曰、天下惡乎定。吾對曰、定於一。孰能一之。對曰、不嗜殺人者能一之。孰能與之。對曰、天下莫不與也。王知夫苗乎。七八月之間旱、則苗槁矣。天油然作雲、沛然下雨、則苗浡然興之矣。其如是、孰能御之。今夫天下之人牧、未有不嗜殺人者也。如有不嗜殺人者、則天下之民皆引領而望之矣。誠如是也、民歸之、由水之就下、沛然誰能御之。

How May the World
Be in Peace

Mencius had been to see King Xiang of Liang. Coming out, he said: 'From a distance, I detected no bearing of a king. Up close, I saw nothing worthy of awe. Brusquely, he asked me: "How may the world be in peace?" I replied: "In unity." "Who could unify?" I replied: "He who has no liking for killing." "Who would follow him?" I replied: "No one would not. Does the King know about sprouts? A drought in summer leaves them withered. If clouds amass and a great rain falls, they spring to life. And then, who can stop their sprouting? Of leaders in the world, not one at present does not like killing. If one of them did not, people far and wide would look up to him. Convinced, they would back him. Like great water gushing down, who could stop their backing?'"

保民而王

齊宣王問曰、齊桓、晉文之事可得聞乎。孟子對曰、仲尼之徒無道恆、文之事者、是以後世無傳焉、臣未之聞也。無以、則王乎。曰、德何如則可以王矣。曰、保民而王、莫之能禦也。曰、若寡人者、可以保民乎哉。曰、可。曰、何由知吾可也。曰、臣聞之胡齕曰、王坐於堂上、有牽牛而過堂下者、王見之、曰、牛何之。對曰、將以釁鐘。王曰、捨之、吾不忍其觳觫、若無罪而就死地。對曰、然則廢釁鐘與。曰、何可廢也、以羊易之。不識有諸。曰、有之。曰、是心足以王矣。百姓皆以王為愛也、臣固知王之不忍也。王曰、然、誠有百姓者。齊國雖褊小、吾何愛一牛。即不忍其觳觫、若無罪而就死地、故以羊易之也。曰、王無異於百姓之以王為愛也。以小易大、彼惡知之。王若隱其無罪而就死地、則牛羊何擇焉。王笑曰、是誠何心哉、我非愛其財、而易之以羊也、宜乎百姓之謂我愛也。曰、無傷也、是乃仁術也、見牛未見羊也。君子之於禽獸也、見其生、不忍見其死、聞其聲、不忍食其肉、是以君子遠庖廚也。王說曰、詩云、他人有心、予忖度之。夫子之謂也。夫我乃行之、反而求之、不得吾心。夫子言之、於我心有戚戚焉。此心之所以合於王者、何也。曰、有複於王者曰、吾力足以舉百鈞、而不足以舉一羽、明足以察秋毫之末、而不見輿薪、則王許之乎。曰、否。今恩足以及禽獸、而功不至於百姓者、獨何與。然則一羽之不舉、為不用力焉、輿薪之不見、為不用明焉、百姓之不見保、為不用恩焉。故王之不王、不為也、非不能也。曰、不為者與不能者之形何以異。曰、挾太山以超北海、語人曰我不能、是誠不能也。為長者折枝、語人曰我不能、是不為也、非不能也。故王之不王、非挾太山以超北海之類也。王之不王、是折枝之類也。老吾老、以及人之老、幼吾幼、以及人之幼、天下可運於掌。詩云、刑於寡妻、至於兄弟、以御於家邦。言舉斯心加諸彼而已。故推恩足以保四海、不推恩無以保妻子。古之人所以大過人者無他焉、善推其所為而已矣。今恩足以及禽獸、而功不至於百姓者、獨何與。權、然後知輕重、度、然後知長短。物皆然、心為甚。王請度之。抑王興甲兵、危士臣、構怨於諸侯、然後快於心與。王曰、否、吾何快於是、將以求吾所大欲也。曰、王之所大欲可得聞與。王笑而不言。曰、為肥甘不足於口與、輕煖不足於體與、抑為采色不足視於目與、聲音不足聽於耳與、便嬖不足使令於前與。王之諸臣皆足以供之、而王豈為是哉。曰、否、吾不為是也。曰、然則王之所大欲可知已。欲辟土地、朝秦楚、莅中國而撫四夷也。以若所為求若所欲、猶緣木而求魚也。王曰、若是其甚與。曰、殆有甚焉。緣木求魚、雖不得魚、無後災。以若所為、求若所欲、盡心力而為之、後必有災。

曰、可得聞與。曰、鄒人與楚人戰、則王以為孰勝。曰、楚人勝。曰、然則小固不可以敵大、寡固不可以敵眾、弱固不可以敵強。海內之地方千里者九、齊集有其一。以一服八、何以異於鄒敵楚哉。蓋亦反其本矣。今王發政施仁、使天下仕者皆欲立於王之朝、耕者皆欲耕於王之野、商賈皆欲藏於王之市、行旅皆欲出於王之塗、天下之欲疾其君者皆欲赴愬於王、其若是、孰能禦之。王曰、吾惽、不能進於是矣。願夫子輔吾志、明以教我。我雖不敏、請嘗試之。曰、無恆產而有恆心者、惟士為能。若民、則無恆產、因無恆心。苟無恆心、放辟、邪侈、無不為已。及陷於罪、然後從而刑之、是罔民也。焉有仁人在位、罔民而可為也。是故明君制民之產、必使仰足以事父母、俯足以畜妻子、樂歲終身飽、凶年免於死亡。然後驅而之善、故民之從之也輕。今也制民之產、仰不足以事父母、俯不足以畜妻子、樂歲終身苦、凶年不免於死亡。此惟救死而恐不贍、奚暇治禮義哉。王欲行之、則盍反其本矣。五畝之宅、樹之以桑、五十者可以衣帛矣。雞豚狗彘之畜、無失其時、七十者可以食肉矣。百畝之田、勿奪其時、八口之家可以無飢矣。謹庠序之教、申之以孝悌之義、頒白者不負戴於道路矣。老者衣帛食肉、黎民不饑不寒、然而不王者、未之有也。

Protect the People

King Xuan of Qi asked Mencius: 'Can I hear about Duke Huan of Qi and Duke Wen of Jin?'

Mencius replied: 'Confucius's disciples did not speak of the dukes. Prosperity has not preserved their tales and I have no knowledge of them. That being so, may I talk about kingly rule through virtue?'

'How might a king rule through virtue?'

'Protect the people, and no one can stop him being the king of all.'

'Can a king such as the benighted protect the people?'

'He can.'

'How do you know that I can?'

'I heard from Hu He that the King was once sitting in the palace when a man leading an ox passed by. The King asked him: "Where is the ox going?" He replied: "To be sacrificed to the bell." The King said: "Let it go! I cannot bear seeing it tremble, an innocent being on its way to die." The man replied: "So we abandon the sacrifice?" The King said: "No. Sacrifice a sheep instead." Did this happen?'

'It did.'

'With such a heart, one can be king of all. People consider the King stingy. I know the King is humane.'

The King said: 'Indeed, some people do. Qi may be small, but how can I be stingy about an ox? I could not bear seeing it tremble, an innocent being on its way to die, so I had a sheep put in its place.'

'The King may not be appalled that people consider him stingy, putting a small animal in a big one's place. What do they know? If the King cannot bear seeing an innnocent being die, what distinguishes an ox from a sheep?'

The King laughed: 'What state of mind is this? I care not for riches, putting a sheep in an ox's place. Yet it makes people think I am stingy.'

'It does no harm. It is an act of benevolence. You saw the ox, not the sheep. Seeing a beast breathe, a gentleman cannot bear seeing it die. Hearing it cry, he cannot bear eating its meat. For this reason, gentlemen stay away from the kitchen.'

Delighted, the King said: 'From the *Odes*: "What goes on in the heart of another, I can surmise." This is you, Sir. For what I did, I find not the reason in my heart. What you say echoes in my heart. Why, with such a heart, can one be king of all?'

'If someone reports to the King, "I have strength enough to lift a hundred *jun*, but not enough to lift a feather; I have vision enough to discern new fur on animals in autumn, but not enough to see a wagon of firewood", does the King approve?'

'No.'

'Now the King has grace enough to extend to the beasts, yet his service has not reached the people. Why exactly? Not lifting a feather, one is not using one's strength. Not seeing a wagon of firewood, one is not using one's vision. People are not protected, for the King has not exercised his grace. Hence, the King has not ruled through virtue because he does not, not because he cannot.'

'How do forms of "does not" and "cannot" differ?'

'Holding Mount Tai under the arm to cross the North Sea and telling people "I cannot", one truly cannot. Bowing to the elderly and telling people "I cannot", one does not – not cannot. Thence, that the King has not ruled through virtue falls not to holding Mount Tai under the arm to cross the North Sea, but to bowing to the elderly. Be gentle to one's elders, and in like manner to others' elders; care for one's children, and in like manner for others' children. Then the world will be held in the palm of your hand. From the *Odes*: "Set an example to your wife and brothers. This keeps safe your family and state". It means we need extend the example to all. Expanding one's grace, one can protect the Four Seas. Not expanding one's grace, one cannot protect one's family. Kings from antiquity surpassed the ordinary, for they extended good deeds to all. Now the King has grace enough to extend to the beasts, yet his service has not reached the people. Why, exactly? Weigh, then we know the weight. Measure, then we know the measure. It is so with things; it is more so with hearts. May the King take account of this! Or does the King wish to mobilise soldiers, jeopardise officials, and antagonise vassals? Would that make him happy?'

The King said: 'No, why would that make me happy? What I do, I do for my great longing.'

'May the King's great longing be

heard?'

The King smiled and said nothing.

Mencius said: 'Are delicacies not enough to the taste? Luxuries not enough to the body? Sceneries not enough for the eye? Music not enough for the ear? Attendants not enough to go around? All this can be provided by the King's courtiers. Does the King wish for this?'

'No, not for this.'

'Then the King's great longing may be known. He longs for his territory to be widened, for Qin and Chu to pay him tribute, for his mandate to be paramount, and for bordering barbarians to be appeased. Doing what you do to pursue your longing resembles fishing atop a tree.'

The King said: 'As bad as this?'

'Worse! Climbing up a tree to fish, one catches no fish but there is no calamity. Doing what you do to pursue your longing, you may give it your all and calamity is surely awaiting.'

'Can the reasoning be heard?'

'Were Zou and Chu to enter a battle, who, in the King's opinion, would win?'

'Chu.'

'As the small cannot fight the big, the few cannot fight the many, the weak cannot fight the strong. Nine states under heaven have a territory larger than a thousand *li*. Assembled, Qi counts as one. As this one challenging the other eight, how does it differ from Zou fighting Chu? Why not return to the elemental? If the King delivers a policy of benevolence, all functionaries shall long to serve in the King's court; all reapers shall long to farm in the King's lands; all merchants shall long to deal in the King's market; all voyagers shall long to travel by the King's roads; all those resenting their sovereigns shall long to confide in the King. If so, who can stop the King?'

The King said: 'I am confounded, and cannot make the grade. I should like to be assisted in my ambition. Enlighten me, Sir. I may not be bright, but do let me try.'

'Possessing no stable property but upholding stable probity, such is a feat proper to scholars. Without stable property, people have no stable morals; without stable morals, they run amok; they then commit crimes and are convicted: this entraps the people. Ruled by a person of benevolence, how could there be such traps? Ergo, a wise sovereign so devises property that people can support their parents and feed their family; with good harvest they eat well and come bad harvest they do not die. Then he urges his people to be kind, and they follow him lightly. People today cannot support their parents nor feed their family; with good harvest they suffer and come bad harvest they die. Survival being the priority, how can they attend to the question of propriety? If the King wishes to exercise a policy of benevolence, why not return to the elemental? Planting mulberry trees around an estate of five *mu*, those aged fifty shall have silk to wear. Not missing the breeding season of domestic animals, those aged seventy shall have meat to eat. Not snatched from a hundred *mu*'s farming season, a family of eight shall not go hungry. Education encouraged and filial piety taught, the elderly shall not be burdened by labour. When the old wear silk and eat meat and when the populace is neither cold nor hungry, and yet their king does not become king of all: now that would be inconceivable.'

乃若其情、則可以爲善矣

公都子曰、告子曰、性無善無不善也。或曰、性可以為善、可以為不善、是故文武興則民好善、幽厲興則民好暴。或曰、有性善有性不善、是故以堯為君而有象、以瞽瞍為父而有舜、以紂為兄之子、且以為君、而有微子啟、王子比干。今曰性善、然則彼皆非與。孟子曰、乃若其情、則可以為善矣、乃所謂善也。若夫為不善、非才之罪也。惻隱之心、人皆有之。羞惡之心、人皆有之。恭敬之心、人皆有之。是非之心、人皆有之。惻隱之心、仁也。羞惡之心、義也。恭敬之心、禮也。是非之心、智也。仁義禮智、非由外鑠我也、我固有之也、弗思耳矣。故曰、求則得之、捨則失之。或相倍蓰而無算者、不能盡其才者也。詩曰、天生蒸民、有物有則、民之秉彝、好是懿德。孔子曰、為此詩者、其知道乎。故有物必有則、民之秉彝也、故好是懿德。

Following Nature, People Are Able to Do Good

Gongduzi said: 'Gaozi thinks human nature has no distinction between good and evil. Some think human nature leads one to do good and evil alike: thus, under King Wen and King Wu, people were partial to goodness; under King You and King Li, people were partial to violence. Some believe that certain are born good, certain born evil: thus, having the enlightened Yao as sovereign there were yet people like Xiang; having a blind man as father there were yet sons like Shun; having the brutal Zhou as nephew, moreover as sovereign, there were yet men like Weizi and Prince Bi Gan. Now you say "Men are born good". Are the others all mistaken?'

Mencius said: 'Following nature, people are able to do good, and that is what I mean. If they do evil, it is not down to their aptitude. Each of us has compassion; each of us knows shame; each of us has respect; each of us knows right and wrong. He who has compassion has benevolence; he who knows shame has honour; he who has respect has propriety; he who knows right and wrong has intellect. Benevolence, honour, propriety and intellect are not imbued but are innate in me; only I had not much thought of it. Hence, "Seek it and one has it; leave it and one loses it". The infinite disparity between men is that of refining or not refining one's gift. From the *Odes*: "Nature gives life; there is matter and there is principle. People abide by nature and aspire to virtue." Confucius said: "He who wrote this was versed in the Tao. Where there is matter, there must be principle. People abide by nature, wherefore they aspire to virtue.'"